AUDIO
ACCESS
INCLUDED

PLAYBACK+
Speed • Pitch • Balance • Loop

VIOLIN

To access audio visit:
www.halleonard.com/mylibrary

Enter Code
1184-7356-9107-5171

ISBN 978-0-634-00074-4

Disney characters and artwork © Disney Enterprises, Inc.

WALT DISNEY MUSIC COMPANY
WONDERLAND MUSIC COMPANY, INC.

DISTRIBUTED BY

HAL•LEONARD®
CORPORATION

7777 W. BLUEMOUND RD. P.O. BOX 13819 MILWAUKEE, WI 53213

Visit Hal Leonard Online at
www.halleonard.com

BE OUR GUEST

from Walt Disney's BEAUTY AND THE BEAST

Lyrics by HOWARD ASHMAN
Music by ALAN MENKEN

VIOLIN

Slowly

Solo Vln.

Play

mf legato

accel.

Fast

f

Slowly

molto rit.

ff

Fast

accel.

f

poco rit.

ff a tempo

4

THE BELLS OF NOTRE DAME

from Walt Disney's THE HUNCHBACK OF NOTRE DAME

Music by ALAN MENKEN
Lyrics by STEPHEN SCHWARTZ

VIOLIN

CAN YOU FEEL THE LOVE TONIGHT

from Walt Disney Pictures' THE LION KING

Music by ELTON JOHN
Lyrics by TIM RICE

VIOLIN

Play

mf

mp

rit.

I JUST CAN'T WAIT TO BE KING

from Walt Disney Pictures' THE LION KING

Music by ELTON JOHN
Lyrics by TIM RICE

VIOLIN

Bright Two-beat

Jungle Flute

COLORS OF THE WIND

from Walt Disney's POCAHONTAS

Music by ALAN MENKEN
Lyrics by STEPHEN SCHWARTZ

VIOLIN

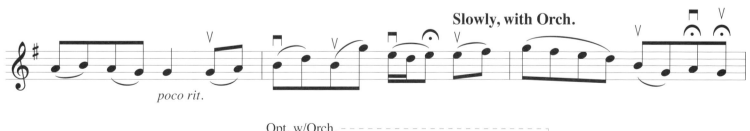

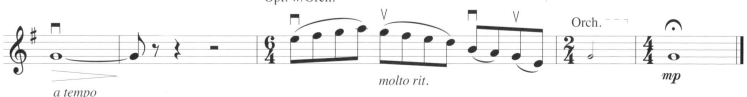

FRIEND LIKE ME

from Walt Disney's ALADDIN

Lyrics by HOWARD ASHMAN
Music by ALAN MENKEN

VIOLIN

Bright Two-beat

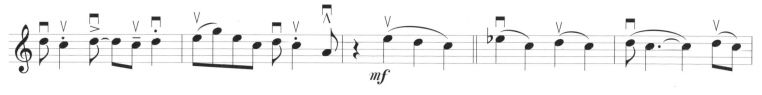

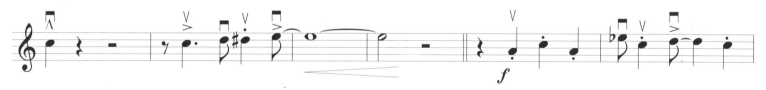

PART OF YOUR WORLD
from Walt Disney's THE LITTLE MERMAID

Lyrics by HOWARD ASHMAN
Music by ALAN MENKEN

VIOLIN

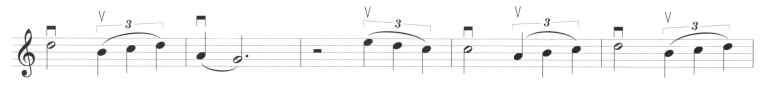

Slower

Tempo I

Play

UNDER THE SEA

from Walt Disney's THE LITTLE MERMAID

Lyrics by HOWARD ASHMAN
Music by ALAN MENKEN

VIOLIN

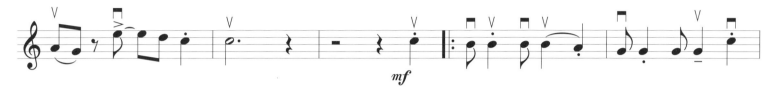

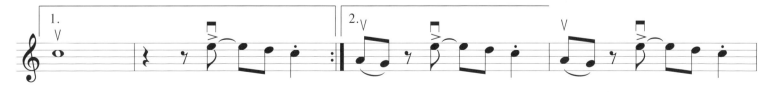

REFLECTION
(Pop Version)
from Walt Disney Pictures' MULAN

Music by MATTHEW WILDER
Lyrics by DAVID ZIPPEL

VIOLIN

Moderately slow

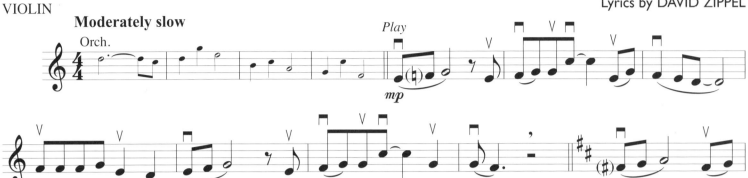

YOU'LL BE IN MY HEART

(Pop Version)

from Walt Disney Pictures' TARZAN™

Words and Music by
PHIL COLLINS

VIOLIN

Moderately

YOU'VE GOT A FRIEND IN ME

from Walt Disney's TOY STORY

Music and Lyrics by
RANDY NEWMAN

VIOLIN

Easy Shuffle

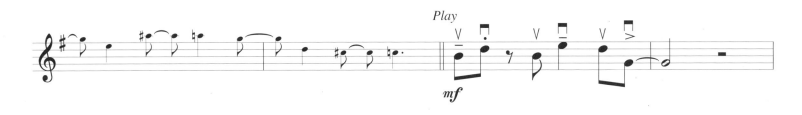

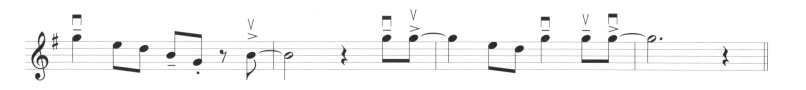

Play

mf

ZERO TO HERO

from Walt Disney Pictures' HERCULES

Music by ALAN MENKEN
Lyrics by DAVID ZIPPEL

VIOLIN

Driving 4

Much faster "a la Baptist Church"